D1523448

How Do Animals use...
Their Voice and sound?

Lynn Stone

Publishing LLC
Vero Beach, Florida 32964

www.rourkepublishing.com

PHOTO CREDITS: All Photos © Lynn Stone, except pg. 21 © Bruse Coleman

Editor: Robert Stengard-Olliges

Cover design by: Nicola Stratford, bdpublishing.com

Library of Congress Cataloging-in-Publication Data

Stone, Lynn M.
  How do animals use their voices and sound? / Lynn Stone.
     p. cm. -- (How do animals use--?)
  ISBN 978-1-60044-507-1
  1. Animal sounds--Juvenile literature. I. Title.
  QL765.S76 2008
  591.59'4--dc22
                                    2007015163

Printed in the USA

CG/CG

Rourke Publishing

www.rourkepublishing.com – rourke@rourkepublishing.com
Post Office Box 3328, Vero Beach, FL 32964

We hear lots of noisy animals.

The **rooster** crows.

5

The **wolf** howls.

7

The panther growls.

9

The **toad** croaks.

11

The baby bird peeps.

The seal barks.

15

The **cow** moos.

The **rattlesnake** rattles its tail.

But **bats** make sounds we can't hear.

Glossary

bat (bat) – a small flying mammal

cow (kou) – an adult female of cattle

rattlesnake (RAT l snayk) – a snake with a tail rattle

22

rooster (ROO stuhr) – an adult male chicken

toad (toad) – looks like a frog but has drier skin

wolf (wulf) – a wild mammal related to dogs

Index

Further Reading

Bullard, Lisa. *Loud and Quiet: An Animal Opposites Book*. At Books, 2006.

Taylor, Thomas. *Loudest Roar*. Oxford, 2005.

Websites

www.kidsites.com/sites-edu/animals.htm

animal.discovery.com

About the Author

Lynn M. Stone is the author of more than 400 children's books. He is a talented natural history photographer as well. Lynn, a former teacher, travels worldwide to photograph wildlife in its natural habitat.